Sadlier We Believe & Pray

Prayers and Practices for Young Catholics

Sadlier

A Division of William H. Sadlier, Inc.

Nihil Obstat
✠ Most Reverend Robert C. Morlino

Imprimatur
✠ Most Reverend Robert C. Morlino
Bishop of Madison
February 26, 2008

The *Nihil Obstat* and *Imprimatur* are official declarations that a book or pamphlet is free of doctrinal or moral error. No implication is contained therein that those who have granted the *Nihil Obstat* and *Imprimatur* agree with the contents, opinions, or statements expressed.

Acknowledgments

Excerpts from the English translation of *The Roman Missal* © 2010, International Committee on English in the Liturgy, Inc. All rights reserved.

Scripture excerpts are taken from the *New American Bible* with *Revised New Testament and Psalms.* Copyright © 1991, 1986, 1970. Confraternity of Christian Doctrine, Inc. Washington, D.C. Used with permission. All rights reserved. No portion of the *New American Bible* may be reprinted without permission in writing from the copyright holder.

Excerpts from the English translation of *Rite of Penance* © 1974, ICEL; excerpts from the English translation of *Order of Christian Funerals* © 1985, ICEL; excerpts from the English translation of *A Book of Prayers* © 1982, ICEL; excerpts from the English translation of *Book of Blessings* © 1988, ICEL. All rights reserved.

Excerpts of the Litany of the Holy Name and Litany of the Saints are taken from *Catholic Household Blessings and Prayers.* Copyright © 1988, United States Conference of Catholic Bishops, Inc., Washington, D.C. (USCCB). Used with permission. All rights reserved.

Excerpts from *Catholic Household Blessings and Prayers* copyright © 1988, United States Conference of Catholic Bishops, Inc., Washington, D.C. (USCCB); excerpts from *Sharing Catholic Social Teaching: Challenges and Directions* © 1998, USCCB; excerpts from the *Compendium: Catechism of the Catholic Church* © 2006, USCCB. Used with permission. All rights reserved.

English translation of the Glory to the Father, *Gloria Patri,* Lord's Prayer, *Pater Noster,* Apostles' Creed, Magnificat, *Gloria in Excelsis,* Nicene Creed, Holy, Holy, Holy, *Sanctus,* Lamb of God, and *Agnus Dei* by the International Consultation on English Texts. (ICET)

Excerpt from the article "Having a Chat with God," adapted from *Christian Prayer for Dummies,* Richard Wagner, © 2002.

Excerpts of prayers for Advent from HYPERLINK "http://www.diocesephoenix.org/catecheticalministry/ADVENT/prayers.htm" www.diocesephoenix.org/catecheticalministry/ADVENT/prayers.htm. Used with permission.

Photo Credits Cover: The Crosiers/Gene Plaisted, OSC. Interior: Alamy/Neil Setchfield: 14. Art Resource, NY/Michael Escoffery/A Child is Born. 1999. Oil on paper. © 2006 Artists Rights Society (ARS), NY: 34 *bottom*; Giraudon: 34 *border.* Jane Bernard: 37. Karen Callaway: 40. Corbis/Richard Gross: 62; Anthony Redpath: 21 *center.* The Crosiers/Gene Plaisted, OSC: 1, 4, 35 *left.* dreamstime: 12, 26–27. Neal Farris: 10, 13 *top,* 15, 20 *center,* 21 *bottom,* 25 *bottom,* 28 *top,* 36, 38, 39, 45, 47, 51 *top* & *center,* 52, 64. frpat.com: 18 *bottom.* Getty Images/Digital Vision/Flying Colours Ltd.: 28 *bottom*; Digital Vision/Jay Freis: 11; Digital Vision/Nancy Ley: 20 *bottom*; Tamara Reynolds: 7; Stone/Denis Waugh: 44–45; Taxi/Ron Chapple: 19; Taxi/Elizabeth Simpson: 57 *background.* Ron Hendricks: 61. iStockphoto/Delafraye Nicolas: 46. Ken Karp: 5, 8, 22 *top,* 23, 25 *top,* 27, 42, 43, 51 *bottom,* 55, 57 *bottom,* 59, 63. Richard Mitchell: 13 *bottom.* PictureQuest/Photodisc/Mel Curtis: 21 *top.* Salesians of Don Bosco: 17 *top.* Shutterstock: 10–11. teresadelosandes.org: 17 *bottom.* The Vatican: 18 *top.* Veer/Rubberball: 20 *top*; Stockbyte: 22 *bottom,* 31, 35 *right,* 50 *left.* W.P. Wittman Ltd.: 38–39, 53.

Illustrator Credits Bernard Adnet: 22. Matthew Archambault: 18 *center.* Luigi Galante: 19. Stephanie Garcia: 14 *top.* Lisa Henderling: 63. Jacey: 31. W. B. Johnston: 47. Michel Larose: 46. Dean Macadam: 48 *bottom left,* 49. Diana Magnuson: 16. Frank Ordaz: 3, 6, 9, 60. Maria Rendon: 58. Tim Robinson: 34. Lauren Scheuer: 11, 24, 44. Neil Slave: 29. Jessica Wolk-Stanley: 48 *bottom right.* Elizabeth Trostli: 14–15. Amanda Warren: 30–31.

William H. Sadlier, Inc.
9 Pine Street
New York, NY 10005-4700

ISBN: 978-0-8215-5700-6

9 10 11 12 IPD 16 15 14 13

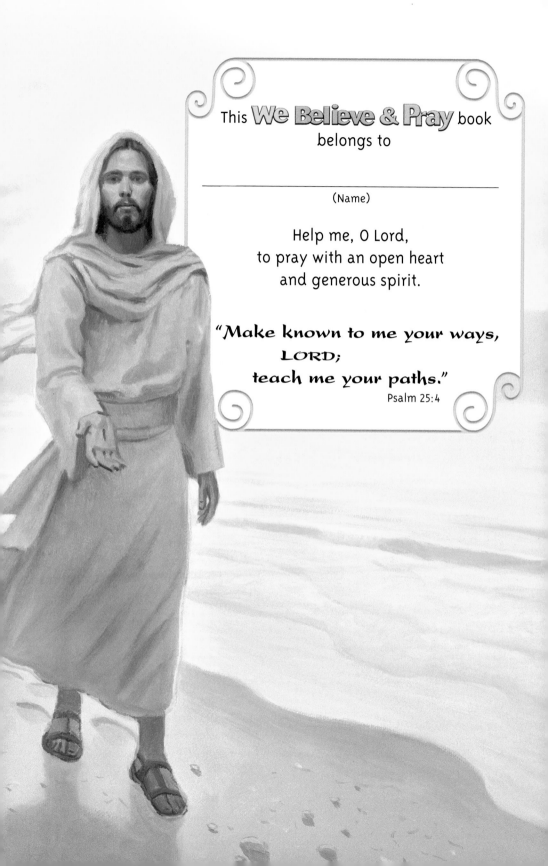

This **We Believe & Pray** book
belongs to

_____

(Name)

Help me, O Lord,
to pray with an open heart
and generous spirit.

"Make known to me your ways,
LORD;
teach me your paths."
Psalm 25:4

Contents

How did Jesus pray?............. 6
Why pray? 7

Catholic Prayers

Praying to the Blessed Trinity
Sign of the Cross
Signum Crucis
Glory to the Father
Gloria Patri 8
Our Father
Pater Noster................................. 9
Litany of the Holy Name 10
Prayer to the Holy Spirit 11

Proclaiming Our Faith in Prayer
Apostles' Creed........................... 12
Act of Faith
Act of Hope
Act of Love 13

Praying with Mary and the Communion of Saints
Hail Mary
Ave Maria.................................. 14
Hail, Holy Queen
Memorare 15
The Angelus 16
Prayer to My Patron Saint
Prayer to Saint John Bosco
Prayer to Saint Teresa de los Andes... 17
Litany of the Saints....................... 18

Asking for God's Blessing
Prayers of Blessing
Psalm 67:2, 7b, 8a
Grace before Meals........................ 19
Prayer for My Family
Prayer on My Birthday
Prayer on My Friend's Birthday....... 20
Prayer for Friendship
Prayer for My Discipleship.............. 21
Prayer for a New School Year 22

Asking for God's Help
Prayers of Petition
Psalm 4:2, 4
Morning Offering 23
Prayer for Stressful Times
Angel of God............................... 24
Prayer for Vocation
Prayer for Decision Making............ 25

Praying for Others
Prayers of Intercession
Prayer for Those Who Are Sick
Prayer for Those Who Have Died 26
Prayer for Peace.......................... 27
Psalm 33:20–22
Prayer before the Game
Athlete's Prayer 28

Thanking God
Prayers of Thanksgiving
Psalm 118:1, 21, 28–29
Prayer after Communion 29
Prayer after Meals
Evening Prayer 30
Prayer for Self-Appreciation 31

Honoring God

Prayers of Praise

Psalm 66:1–3a
Psalm 23:1–4 32
Divine Praises 33
The Magnificat 34

Catholic Life & Practices

Celebrating the Sacraments

Sacraments of Christian Initiation
Sacraments of Healing
Sacraments at the Service
    of Communion 35

Prayers from the Celebration of the Eucharist

Confiteor
Gloria.. 36
Nicene Creed 37
Holy, Holy, Holy
Sanctus, Sanctus, Sanctus 38
Memorial Acclamation
Lamb of God
Agnus Dei 39

Praying before the Most Blessed Sacrament

Visit to the Most Blessed Sacrament
Benediction 40

The Sacrament of Penance and Reconciliation

Four Parts of the Sacrament 41
Examination of Conscience 42
Act of Contrition 43

Living as a Disciple

The Ten Commandments 44
The Great Commandment 45
The Beatitudes 46
The Works of Mercy 47
The Precepts of the Church
Holy Days of Obligation 48
Catholic Social Teaching 49

Some Popular Devotions

The Rosary................................... 50
Stations of the Cross 52
First Friday Devotions 54

Praying with Scripture

Lectio Divina 55

the Liturgical year

Advent 56
Christmas
Prayer to the Holy Family 57
Ordinary Time 58
Lent 59
Triduum
    Holy Thursday 60
    Good Friday 61
    Easter Vigil 62
Easter.. 63
Ascension
Pentecost 64

How did Jesus pray?

Jesus prayed . . .
- alone
- with family
- with friends
- with his Jewish community
- with his disciples
- with the teachers

Jesus prayed everywhere . . .
- in the mountains
- in the desert
- in the synagogue
- at the shore
- on his road journeys

Jesus prayed by . . .
- quietly focusing on God
- studying Scriptures
- praying the psalms
- giving thanks to his Father
- healing people
- forgiving people
- talking to God about his feelings

Why pray?

Turn to God in prayer for . . .

- guidance and direction
- help to know and follow his will
- courage to be a strong believer

5 forms of prayer are . . .

- **blessing**—dedicating someone or something to God or making something holy in God's name
- **petition**—asking something of God, such as forgiveness
- **intercession**—asking for something on behalf of another person or a group of people
- **thanksgiving**—showing gratitude to God for all he has given us
- **praise**—giving glory to God for being God

Take time in prayer to . . .

- speak to God
- listen to God
- share your thoughts, dreams, and needs

Who prays?

89% of teenagers pray in a normal week

95% of adults thank God for what he has done in their lives

76% ask for forgiveness for specific sins

61% ask for help for specific needs

47% are silent during prayer to listen for God

52% who pray do so several times a day

13% of Catholics have extended prayer time with other family members

33% of adults regularly participate in prayer group

Find out more about prayer:

ONLINE COMPONENTS
www.webelieveandpray.com

Catholic ✝ Prayers

Did you Know?

Today, Catholics around the world celebrate the Mass and other sacraments in their own languages. But the ancient language called Latin is still the official language of the Roman Catholic Church. Does your parish or any parish in your area offer Masses celebrated in Latin?

Sign of *the Cross*

In the name of the Father,
and of the Son,
and of the Holy Spirit. Amen.

 Latin

In nomine Patris
et Filii
et Spiritus Sancti. Amen.

Glory to *the Father*

Glory to the Father, and to the Son,
    and to the Holy Spirit:
as it was in the beginning,
    is now, and will be for ever.
Amen.

 Latin

Gloria Patri
et Filio
et Spiritui Sancto.
Sicut erat in principio,
et nunc et semper
et in sæcula sæculorum. Amen.

Our *Father*

Our Father, who art in heaven,
hallowed be thy name;
thy kingdom come;
thy will be done on earth
    as it is in heaven.
Give us this day our
    daily bread;
and forgive us our
    trespasses
as we forgive those who
    trespass against us;
and lead us not
    into temptation,
but deliver us from
    evil.
    Amen.

Pater noster qui es in cælis:
sanctificetur Nomen Tuum;
adveniat Regnum Tuum;
fiat voluntas Tua,
sicut in cælo, et in terra.
Panem nostrum
cotidianum da nobis hodie;
et dimitte nobis debita nostra,
sicut et nos
dimittimus debitoribus nostris;
et ne nos inducas in tentationem;
sed libera nos a Malo.
Amen.

For Latin pronunciation:

ONLINE COMPONENTS
www.webelieveandpray.com

More About

The Lord's Prayer

Jesus' disciples once said to him, "Lord, teach us to pray" (Luke 11:1). Jesus then taught them a very special prayer to God the Father called the Lord's Prayer. It is one of the most important prayers in the Gospels and of the Church. It is also known as the Our Father. As followers of Jesus Christ, we pray the Lord's Prayer at each Mass and at many other times in our lives.

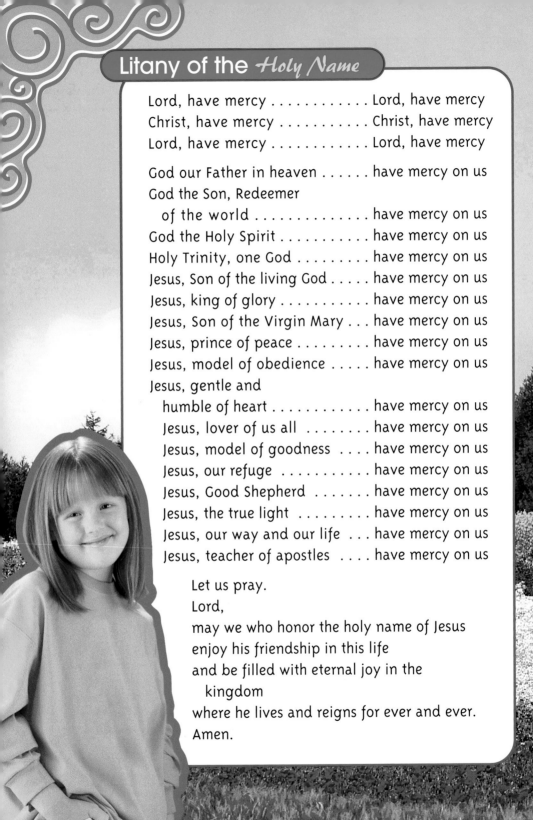

Litany of the *Holy Name*

Lord, have mercy	Lord, have mercy
Christ, have mercy	Christ, have mercy
Lord, have mercy	Lord, have mercy

God our Father in heaven . . . . . . have mercy on us
God the Son, Redeemer
  of the world . . . . have mercy on us
God the Holy Spirit . . . . have mercy on us
Holy Trinity, one God . . . . have mercy on us
Jesus, Son of the living God . . . . . have mercy on us
Jesus, king of glory . . . . have mercy on us
Jesus, Son of the Virgin Mary . . . have mercy on us
Jesus, prince of peace . . . . have mercy on us
Jesus, model of obedience . . . . . have mercy on us
Jesus, gentle and
  humble of heart . . . . have mercy on us
  Jesus, lover of us all . . . . have mercy on us
  Jesus, model of goodness . . . . have mercy on us
  Jesus, our refuge . . . . have mercy on us
  Jesus, Good Shepherd . . . . have mercy on us
  Jesus, the true light . . . . have mercy on us
  Jesus, our way and our life . . . have mercy on us
  Jesus, teacher of apostles . . . . have mercy on us

Let us pray.
Lord,
may we who honor the holy name of Jesus
enjoy his friendship in this life
and be filled with eternal joy in the
  kingdom
where he lives and reigns for ever and ever.
Amen.

Come *Holy Spirit*

Come, Holy Spirit, fill the hearts of your faithful.
And kindle in them the fire of your love.

Send forth your Spirit and they shall be created.
And you will renew the face of the earth.

Let us pray.

Lord,
by the light of the Holy Spirit
you have taught the hearts of your
     faithful.
In the same Spirit
help us to relish what is right
and always rejoice in your
     consolation.
We ask this through Christ our Lord.
Amen.

Apostles' Creed

I believe in God, the Father almighty,
   Creator of heaven and earth,

and in Jesus Christ, his only Son,
   our Lord,
who was conceived by the Holy Spirit,
born of the Virgin Mary,
suffered under Pontius Pilate,
was crucified, died and was buried;
he descended into hell;
on the third day he rose again
from the dead;
he ascended into heaven,
and is seated at the right hand
   of God the Father almighty;
from there he will come to judge
   the living and the dead.

I believe in the Holy Spirit,
   the holy catholic Church,
   the communion of saints,
   the forgiveness of sins,
   the resurrection of the body,
   and life everlasting. Amen.

Who were They?

We learn about the names of Jesus' Apostles in the New Testament. "The names of the twelve apostles are these: first, Simon called Peter, and his brother Andrew; James, the son of Zebedee, and his brother John; Philip and Bartholomew, Thomas and Matthew the tax collector; James, the son of Alphaeus, and Thaddeus; Simon the Cananean, and Judas Iscariot who betrayed him." (Matthew 10:2–4) Here are some other facts we learn: Peter and Andrew were fishermen. Thomas was a twin. John had a temper. For this reason, Jesus called him the "son of thunder." James was the brother of John and was the first Apostle to die for his faith. Do you know more about the Apostles?

Act of *Faith*

O my God, I firmly believe that you are one God in three divine Persons, Father, Son, and Holy Spirit. I believe that your divine Son became man and died for our sins and that he will come to judge the living and the dead. I believe these and all the truths which the Holy Catholic Church teaches because you have revealed them who are eternal truth and wisdom, who can neither deceive nor be deceived. In this faith I intend to live and die. Amen.

Did you Know?

The theological virtues of faith, hope, and love are often illustrated by three symbols: a cross, an anchor, and a heart. The cross on which Jesus gave up his life for us is a universal symbol of our Christian faith. In the New Testament hope is called an "anchor of the soul" (Hebrews 6:19). And the heart is recognized by people everywhere as a symbol of love. Have you seen these symbols used in your parish?

Act of *Hope*

O Lord God, I hope by your grace for the pardon of all my sins and after life here to gain eternal happiness because you have promised it who are infinitely powerful, faithful, kind, and merciful. In this hope I intend to live and die. Amen.

Act of *Love*

O Lord God, I love you above all things and I love my neighbor for your sake because you are the highest, infinite and perfect good, worthy of all my love. In this love I intend to live and die. Amen.

13

Hail *Mary*

Latin

Hail Mary, full of grace,
the Lord is with you!
Blessed are you among women,
and blessed is the fruit
    of your womb, Jesus.
Holy Mary, Mother of God,
pray for us sinners,
now and at the hour of our death.
Amen.

Ave, Maria, gratia plena,
Dominus tecum.
Benedicta tu in mulieribus,
et benedictus fructus ventris
    tui, Iesus.
Sancta Maria, Mater Dei,
ora pro nobis peccatoribus,
nunc et in hora mortis nostræ.
Amen.

Hail,  Holy Queen

Hail, holy Queen, mother of mercy,
hail, our life, our sweetness, and our hope.
To you we cry, the children of Eve;
to you we send up our sighs,
mourning and weeping in this land of exile.
Turn, then, most gracious advocate,
your eyes of mercy toward us;
lead us home at last
and show us the blessed fruit of your womb,
  Jesus:
O clement, O loving, O sweet Virgin Mary.

Memorare

Remember, most loving Virgin Mary,
never was it heard
that anyone who turned to you for help
was left unaided.

Inspired by this confidence,
though burdened by my sins,
I run to your protection
for you are my mother.
Mother of the Word of God,
do not despise my words of pleading
but be merciful and hear my prayer.
Amen.

The *Angelus*

The angel spoke God's message to Mary,
and she conceived of the Holy Spirit.
Hail, Mary . . .

"I am the lowly servant of the Lord:
let it be done to me according to your
    word."
Hail, Mary . . .

And the Word became flesh
and lived among us.
Hail, Mary . . .

Pray for us, holy Mother of God,
that we may become worthy of the
    promises of Christ.

Let us pray.
Lord,
fill our hearts with your grace:
once, through the message of an angel
you revealed to us the incarnation of
    your Son;
now, through his suffering and death
lead us to the glory of his resurrection.

We ask this through Christ our Lord.
Amen.

Prayer *to my Patron Saint*

Dear Saint _____,
(Name)

In (Baptism/Confirmation) your name
became mine, and you became my patron.
Please pray for me as I live my life each day,
and help me to honor you by following
your example of faithfulness to Jesus.
Amen.

Prayer *to Saint John Bosco*

Dear Saint John Bosco, patron of young people,
during your life you helped many young people
learn to love Jesus.
You found them places where they could meet
to pray, learn, and play together.
You taught them about Jesus and his love for them.
Help me to live my life as you did, showing my
love for Jesus in everything I say and do.
Amen.

Prayer *to Saint Teresa de los Andes*

Dear Saint Teresa de los Andes,
patron of young people,
you showed your great love for God in every
action of your life.
You lived as a model of holiness at home, at
school, and among your friends.
You were loved and admired by everyone you
knew, but you loved and admired Jesus above all.
Help me live each day of my life as you did yours,
in joy and love for God.
Amen.

Litany of the Saints

Lord, have mercy . . . . Lord, have mercy

Christ, have mercy . . . . Christ, have mercy

Lord, have mercy . . . . Lord, have mercy

Holy Mary, Mother
of God . . . . pray for us

Saint John the Baptist . . . . . pray for us

Saint Joseph . . . . pray for us

Saint Peter and
Saint Paul . . . . pray for us

Saint Andrew . . . . pray for us

Saint John . . . . pray for us

Saint Mary Magdalene . . . . pray for us

Saint Ignatius of
Antioch . . . . pray for us

Saint Francis and
Saint Dominic . . . . pray for us

Saint Catherine . . . . pray for us

Saint Teresa . . . . pray for us

All holy men
and women . . . . pray for us

Let us pray.

In this age we would be counted
in this communion of all the saints;
keep us always in their good and
blessed company.

In their midst we make every prayer
through Christ who is our Lord for
ever and ever.

Amen.

St. María de Jesús
Sacramentado

St. Charles Lwanga

Did you Know?

The Church has a special process to honor people who have lived holy lives and have witnessed to Jesus Christ. This process is called *canonization*. Church leaders examine the life of each person whose name has been submitted for sainthood. They gather proof that this person has lived a life of faith and holiness. When a person is canonized, the Church officially names him or her a saint. We remember each canonized saint on a special day during the Church year.

St. Peregrine

Psalm 67

May God be gracious to us and bless us;
  may God's face shine upon us.
  God, our God, blesses us.
May God bless us still.

Psalm 67:2, 7b, 8a

Grace *before Meals*

Bless † us, O Lord, and these your gifts
which we are about to receive from
  your goodness.
Through Christ our Lord.
Amen.

Prayers of Blessing

God continually blesses us with many gifts. Because God first blessed us, we, too, can pray for his blessings on people and things. "The grace of the Lord Jesus Christ and the love of God and the fellowship of the holy Spirit be with all of you." (2 Corinthians 13:13) When have you been blessed?

Prayer *for My Family*

O God,
shower your blessings on this family
    gathered here in your name.
Enable those who are joined by one
    love to support one another
by their fervor of spirit and devotion
    to prayer.
Make them responsive to the needs
    of others and witnesses to the faith
    in all they say and do. Amen.

Prayer *on My Birthday*

Dear God,
today I begin a new year of my life.
Help me to remember that the greatest
    gifts I receive today and every day are
    your gifts of life and love.
Help me to use these gifts to make a
    difference in the world and to grow
    to be a better person. Amen.

Prayer *on My Friend's Birthday*

Loving God,
you created all the people of the world,
    and you know each of us by name.
We thank you for (name),
    who celebrates his/her birthday.
Bless him/her with your love and friendship
    that he/she may grow in wisdom,
        knowledge, and grace.
May he/she love his/her family always
    and be ever faithful to his/her friends. Amen.

Prayer *for Friendship*

Jesus, help me to follow your example in
being a good and faithful friend.
Help me to show respect for my friends in
the way that I speak to them and in the
way that I listen to them.
Help me to remember to share kind words with
friends when they are hurt or feeling sad.
When we spend time together,
help my friends and me to remember that
you are present with us. Amen.

Prayer *for My Discipleship*

Jesus, you invite me to be your disciple.
You showed me how to love God the Father
with all my heart, with all my soul, and with
all my mind.
You showed me how to love my neighbors
and the importance of loving myself.

It is not always easy to be a disciple.
I am grateful for the example you have
given to me.
Jesus, continue to guide me
and strengthen me on my journey
to be your disciple. Amen.

Prayer *for a New School Year*

Dear God,
each new school year brings new beginnings,
new opportunities for me to learn, grow,
and make friends.
Be with me each day as I am faced with many
challenges.
Help me in accepting new classmates and in
showing respect for my teachers.
Help me to do my best—both in and out
of school.
Guide me and my classmates as we journey
together in the months ahead.
Amen.

Meet
Joshua

Age: 12

Town: Fort Collins, Colorado

My Goals: to get good grades, especially in Math; to make it on the basketball team, to make new friends

My Worries: that I won't fit in with my new classmates, that I won't understand the new work, that I won't find a new best friend

My Happiness: playing basketball, going to the park

My Question: Why did my family have to move away?

Psalm 4

Answer when I call, my saving God.
   In my troubles, you cleared a way;
   show me favor; hear my prayer.

Know that the LORD works wonders
      for the faithful;
   the LORD hears when I call out.

Psalm 4:2, 4

Prayers of Petition

Jesus prayed prayers of petition in which he asked God the Father for help in doing his will. For example on the night before he died, Jesus prayed, "Father, if you are willing, take this cup away from me; still, not my will but yours be done" (Luke 22:42). Have you prayed to God for help recently?

Morning *Offering*

O Jesus, I offer you all my prayers,
   works, and sufferings of this day
for all the intentions of your most
   Sacred Heart.
Amen.

Write your own Morning Offering here.

My Morning *Offering*

Dear Jesus,

_____

_____

_____

_____

_____

23

Prayer for **Stressful** Times

Dear God,
when there is so much happening around
me—school, work, practice, and
   responsibilities—
I sometimes feel so overwhelmed.
I ask myself . . .
Can I accomplish what has to be done?
Will I reach my goals?
Will I come through for those counting
   on me?
How can I always do my best?

Father,
during these times that I feel stressed,
help me to remember what is most
   important.
Help me to depend on you for strength
and to find time to focus on you.
Knowing that you are with me helps me
   to be strong enough to get through
      this stressful time. Amen.

Angel of God

Angel of God,
my guardian dear,
to whom God's love commits me here,
ever this day be at my side,
to light and guard, to rule and guide.
Amen.

I didn't Know

The word *angel* comes from a Greek word that means "messenger." Angels were created by God as pure spirits with no physical bodies. All through the Bible, we find angels carrying God's messages to his people. We also read that God gives us angels to watch over us.
(See Acts of the Apostles 12:1–11.)

Prayer for Vocation

Dear God,
you have a great and loving plan
for our world and for me.
I wish to share in that plan fully,
faithfully, and joyfully.

Help me to understand what it is
you wish me to do with my life.
Help me to be attentive to the
signs that you give me about
preparing for the future.

Help me to learn to be a sign
of the Kingdom of God
whether I am called to the priesthood
or religious life, the single or married life.

And once I have heard and understood
your call, give me the strength
and the grace to follow it
with generosity and love. Amen.

Prayer for Decision Making

Jesus,
I know that I am supposed to consider
you in every decision I make.
But I sometimes decide on what I think is
best for me, without considering its
effect on others.

Help me to remember your example
when I have a decision to make. Help
me to decide to do the right thing and
to remember you as I make my choice.
Guide my actions so they may have a
positive effect on others. Amen.

Prayer *for Those Who Are Sick*

Lord Jesus,
who went about doing good and healing all,
we ask you to bless your friends who are sick.

Dear Jesus,
when you were on earth, you touched and
    healed so many people.
You bring comfort to the sick.
Please bring your healing love to (name)
    who is sick.
Amen.

Prayer *for Those Who Have Died*

Eternal rest grant unto them, O Lord,
and let perpetual light shine upon them.

May they rest in peace.
Amen.

May their souls and the souls of all the faithful
    departed,
through the mercy of God, rest in peace.
Amen.

Prayers of Intercession

Jesus prayed prayers of intercession, prayers
for the needs of other people. Even as he hung
on the cross he prayed, "Father, forgive them,
they know not what they do" (Luke 23:34).
Who needs your prayers today?

More About Peace

In 1963 Blessed Pope John XXIII wrote to the entire Church and to people of good will around the world. He called the letter *Pacem in Terris*, which is Latin for "Peace on Earth." In it he reminded us that the world will never be the dwelling place of peace until the peace of Christ has found a home in each of us.

Prayer *for Peace*

Lord, make me an instrument
   of your peace:
where there is hatred, let me sow love;
where there is injury, pardon;
where there is doubt, faith;
where there is despair, hope;
where there is darkness, light;
where there is sadness, joy.

O divine Master, grant that I
   may not so much seek
to be consoled as to console,
to be understood as to understand,
to be loved as to love.
For it is in giving that we receive,
it is in pardoning that we are
   pardoned,
it is in dying that we are born to
   eternal life.
Amen.

Psalm 33

Our soul waits for the LORD,
    who is our help and shield.
For in God our hearts rejoice;
    in your holy name we trust.
May your kindness, LORD, be upon us;
    we have put our hope in you.

Psalm 33:20–22

Prayer *before the Game*

God,
please be with me and my teammates
    as we prepare for our game.
Help us to do our best,
and to remember the skills we have practiced.
Help us to work together to achieve our goal,
    whether we win or lose.

God, be with our opponents also.
They too have worked hard.
Help us to remember to be good
    teammates and competitors
and keep us safe as we play. Amen.

Athlete's *Prayer*

God, thank you for the abilities you give me
    to play my sport.
Jesus, be with me as I play
    that I might do my best.
Holy Spirit, inspire me as I compete.
May I always play fairly and with respect
    for my opponents.
Whatever the outcome of this game, bless me,
    Father, Son, and Holy Spirit. Amen.

Psalm *118*

Give thanks to the LORD, who is good,
    whose love endures forever.
I thank you for you answered me;
    you have been my savior.
You are my God, I give you thanks;
    my God, I offer you praise.
Give thanks to the LORD, who is good,
    whose love endures forever.

Psalm 118:1, 21, 28–29

Prayer *after Communion*

Jesus,
thank you for coming to me in
    Communion.
Thank you for strengthening me
    to be your disciple and to serve
      others.
Help me to be grateful for each day
    and to stay close to you always.
Amen.

Prayers of Thanksgiving

Jesus prayed prayers of thanksgiving.
He once prayed "Father, I thank you for
hearing me. I know that you always
hear me" (John 11:41–42). When
have you said a prayer of thanks?

Prayer *after Meals*

We give you thanks for all your gifts,
   almighty God,
living and reigning now and for ever.
Amen.

Evening *Prayer*

Dear God, before I sleep
I want to thank you for this day,
so full of your kindness and your joy.
I close my eyes to rest
safe in your loving care.

Write your own Evening Prayer here.

My Evening *Prayer*

_____

_____

_____

_____

_____

_____

_____

Prayer *for Self-Appreciation*

Dear God,
I know you created me out of love.
You love me no matter what—just the way I am.
God, you see my hidden talents and know what I can do.
Sometimes I am not happy being me.
Help me to see myself as you see me.
Amen.

Q: Have you ever discovered something about yourself that surprised you?

A: Last week I was working on a group project at school. My teacher assigned each group to design and draw banners and posters for an event the school was going to have. After I finished my poster, my group kept saying "WOW! That's great!" I even won the Best Design ribbon! I didn't even think about drawing as a talent because I had fun doing this project. Now I want to ask my mom about taking a special art class on Saturday mornings. There's so much I want to learn.

Ethan, 12 years old, Rhode Island

Prayers of Praise

Jesus sometimes prayed prayers of praise. He praised his Father as the source of everything that is good. He once prayed, "I give praise to you, Father, Lord of heaven and earth" (Matthew 11:25). What words of praise will you pray?

Psalm 66

Shout joyfully to God, all you on earth;
sing of his glorious name;
give him glorious praise.
Say to God: "How awesome your deeds!"

Psalm 66:1–3a

Psalm 23

The LORD is my shepherd;
there is nothing I lack.
In green pastures you let me graze;
to safe waters you lead me;
you restore my strength.
You guide me along the right path
for the sake of your name.
Even when I walk through a dark valley,
I fear no harm for you are at my side;
your rod and staff give me courage.

Psalm 23:1–4

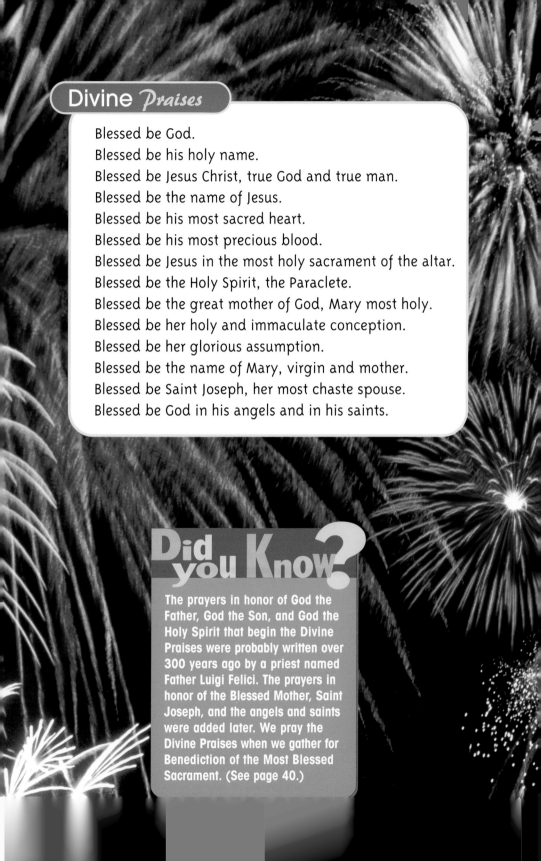

Divine *Praises*

Blessed be God.
Blessed be his holy name.
Blessed be Jesus Christ, true God and true man.
Blessed be the name of Jesus.
Blessed be his most sacred heart.
Blessed be his most precious blood.
Blessed be Jesus in the most holy sacrament of the altar.
Blessed be the Holy Spirit, the Paraclete.
Blessed be the great mother of God, Mary most holy.
Blessed be her holy and immaculate conception.
Blessed be her glorious assumption.
Blessed be the name of Mary, virgin and mother.
Blessed be Saint Joseph, her most chaste spouse.
Blessed be God in his angels and in his saints.

Did you Know?

The prayers in honor of God the Father, God the Son, and God the Holy Spirit that begin the Divine Praises were probably written over 300 years ago by a priest named Father Luigi Felici. The prayers in honor of the Blessed Mother, Saint Joseph, and the angels and saints were added later. We pray the Divine Praises when we gather for Benediction of the Most Blessed Sacrament. (See page 40.)

The *Magnificat*

(Canticle of Mary)

My soul proclaims the greatness of the Lord,
my spirit rejoices in God my Savior;
for he has looked with favor on his lowly servant.
From this day all generations will call me blessed:
the Almighty has done great things for me,
and holy is his Name.
He has mercy on those who fear him
in every generation.
He has shown the strength of his arm,
he has scattered the proud in their conceit.
He has cast down the mighty from their thrones,
and has lifted up the lowly.
He has filled the hungry with good things,
and the rich he has sent away empty.
He has come to the help of his servant Israel
for he has remembered his promise of mercy,
the promise he made to our fathers,
to Abraham and his children for ever.

A Child Is Born, ©2007
Michael Escoffery, Artists
Rights Society (ARS), NY

Catholic Life & Practices

Celebrating the Sacraments

The Sacraments of Baptism, Confirmation, and Eucharist are called the *Sacraments of Christian Initiation*. Through these sacraments we are born into the Church, strengthened, and nourished.

The Sacraments of Penance and Reconciliation and Anointing of the Sick are known as the *Sacraments of Healing*. Through these sacraments we experience God's forgiveness, peace, and healing.

The Sacraments of Holy Orders and Matrimony are called *Sacraments at the Service of Communion*. Through these sacraments we are strengthened to serve God and the Church through service to others.

Sacraments of Christian Initiation

 Baptism

 Confirmation

 Eucharist

Sacraments of Healing

 Penance and Reconciliation

 Anointing of the Sick

Sacraments at the Service of Communion

 Holy Orders

 Matrimony

Prayers from the Celebration

Confiteor

I confess to almighty God
and to you, my brothers and sisters,
that I have greatly sinned,
in my thoughts and in my words,
in what I have done and in what I have failed to do,
through my fault, through my fault,
through my most grievous fault;
therefore I ask blessed Mary ever-Virgin,
all the Angels and Saints,
and you, my brothers and sisters,
to pray for me to the Lord our God.

Gloria

Glory to God in the highest,
and on earth peace to people of good will.

We praise you, we bless you,
we adore you, we glorify you,
we give you thanks for your great glory,
Lord God, heavenly King, O God, almighty Father.

Lord Jesus Christ, Only Begotten Son,
Lord God, Lamb of God, Son of the Father,
you take away the sins of the world, have mercy on us;
you take away the sins of the world, receive our prayer;
you are seated at the right hand of the Father, have mercy on us.

For you alone are the Holy One,
you alone are the Lord,
you alone are the Most High,
Jesus Christ,
with the Holy Spirit,
in the glory of God the Father.
Amen.

Nicene *Creed*

I believe in one God,
    the Father almighty,
    maker of heaven and earth,
    of all things visible and invisible.

I believe in one Lord Jesus Christ,
    the Only Begotten Son of God,
    born of the Father before all ages.
    God from God, Light from Light,
    true God from true God,
    begotten, not made, consubstantial
      with the Father;
    through him all things were made.
    For us men and for our salvation
      he came down from heaven,
and by the Holy Spirit
    was incarnate of the Virgin Mary,
      and became man.
For our sake he was crucified
      under Pontius Pilate,
    he suffered death and was buried,
    and rose again on the third day
      in accordance with the Scriptures.

He ascended into heaven
    and is seated at the right hand
    of the Father.
He will come again in glory to judge
    the living and the dead
and his kingdom will have no end.

I believe in the Holy Spirit, the Lord,
    the giver of life,
    who proceeds from the Father and
    the Son,
who with the Father and the Son
    is adored and glorified,
who has spoken through the prophets.
I believe in one, holy, catholic
    and apostolic Church.
I confess one Baptism for the
    forgiveness of sins
and I look forward to the
    resurrection of the dead
and the life of the world to come.
Amen.

Did you Know?

The prayers on pages 36–39 are from the Mass. There are four parts of the Mass: the Introductory Rites, the Liturgy of the Word, the Liturgy of the Eucharist, and the Concluding Rites. The prayers on pages 38–39 are all prayed during the Liturgy of the Eucharist.

Holy, *Holy, Holy*

Holy, Holy, Holy Lord
  God of hosts.
Heaven and earth are full of your glory.
    Hosanna in the highest.
Blessed is he who comes in
  the name of the Lord.
    Hosanna in the highest.

Latin

Sanctus, Sanctus, Sanctus Dominus
  Deus Sabaoth.
Pleni sunt cæli et terra gloria tua.
    Hosanna in excelsis.
Benedictus qui venit in nomine
  Domini.
    Hosanna in excelsis.

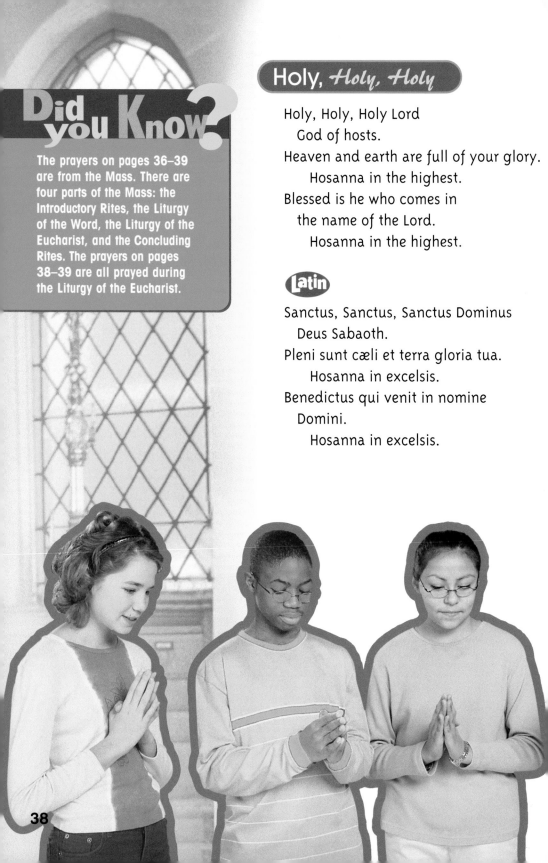

38

Memorial *Acclamation*

We proclaim your Death, O Lord,
and profess your Resurrection
until you come again.

Lamb *of God*

Lamb of God, you take away the
    sins of the world,
  have mercy on us.
Lamb of God, you take away the
    sins of the world,
  have mercy on us.
Lamb of God, you take away the
    sins of the world,
  grant us peace.

Latin

Agnus Dei, qui tollis peccata mundi:
    miserere nobis.
Agnus Dei, qui tollis peccata mundi:
    miserere nobis.
Agnus Dei, qui tollis peccata mundi:
    dona nobis pacem.

Visit *to the Most Blessed Sacrament*

After Communion at Mass, the consecrated Hosts that remain are placed in the tabernacle. A special light, called the *sanctuary lamp*, is always kept burning nearby. This light reminds us that Jesus Christ is present in the Most Blessed Sacrament. We show reverence for Jesus, who is really present in the Eucharist. We do this by *genuflecting*, or bending the right knee to the floor, toward the tabernacle.

We often go into church at times other than the celebration of Mass and the sacraments to "make a visit"—to take time to tell Jesus of our love, our needs, our hopes, and our thanks.

Benediction

Benediction is a very old practice in the Church. The word *benediction* comes from the Latin word for "blessing."

At Benediction a large Host, that was consecrated during Mass, is placed in a special holder called a *monstrance* (comes from a Latin word meaning "to show") so that all can see the Most Blessed Sacrament. Benediction includes hymns, a blessing, and praying the Divine Praises (see page 33). The priest burns incense before the Most Blessed Sacrament. The incense is a sign of the adoration and prayer we offer in God's presence.

This beautiful devotion of Benediction reminds us that Jesus fills our lives with blessings.

The Sacrament of Penance and Reconciliation

Four Parts *of the Sacrament*

Contrition

- We express heartfelt sorrow.

- We tell God we are truly sorry for our sins and firmly intend not to sin again.

- We pray an act of contrition.

Confession

- We tell or confess our sins to the priest.

- We talk with the priest about ways to love God and others.

Penance

- The priest asks us to say a prayer or perform a good act that shows sorrow for sins. This prayer or action is a *penance*. It helps to make up for any harm caused by sin and to grow as a disciple of Christ.

Absolution

- We are given God's forgiveness of our sins through the words and actions of the priest.

Examination of Conscience

Here are some questions to help you reflect on your relationship with God and others. You might review the Ten Commandments (page 44) and the Beatitudes (page 46).

Love God with all your heart

- Do I make anyone or anything more important to me than God? Have I read from the Bible and prayed?
- Do I respect God's name and the name of Jesus?
- Do I participate in Mass on Sunday and keep Sunday as a day of rest?

Love others

- Do I show obedience to God by obeying my parents, guardians, and teachers?
- Have I hurt others by my words and actions? Have I helped those in need?
- Have I been selfish or taken the belongings of others without their permission? Have I shared my belongings?
- Have I been happy for others when they have the things they want or need?

Love yourself

- Do I respect myself? Do I take good care of my body and show respect to others? Do I respect the dignity of everyone I meet?
- Have I been honest? Have I lied or cheated?
- Do I speak, act, and dress in ways that show respect for myself and others?

How am I Doing?

When we examine our conscience, we think about whether the choices we have made showed love for God, ourselves, and others. We ask ourselves whether we have sinned, either by doing something that we know is against God's law, or by not doing something that God's law calls us to do.

Act of Contrition

My God,
I am sorry for my sins with all my heart.
In choosing to do wrong
and failing to do good,
I have sinned against you
whom I should love above all things.
I firmly intend, with your help,
to do penance,
to sin no more,
and to avoid whatever leads me to sin.
Our Savior Jesus Christ
suffered and died for us.
In his name, my God, have mercy.

More About Acts of Contrition

An Act of Contrition is a prayer in which we express sorrow for our wrongdoings. We pray an Act of Contrition during the Sacrament of Penance. We can also pray it anytime we want to ask God's forgiveness. You can pray the Act of Contrition on this page or any other Act of Contrition. You can also use your own words of sorrow such as: "Lord Jesus, Son of God, have mercy on me, a sinner."

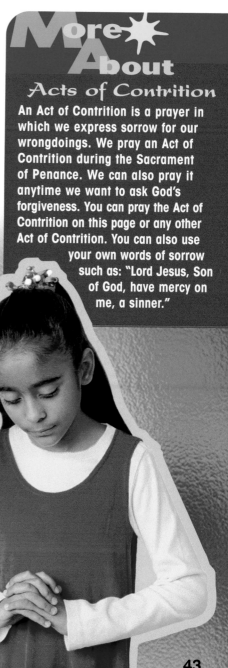

Living as a Disciple

The *Ten* Commandments

1. I am the LORD your God: you shall not have strange gods before me.

2. You shall not take the name of the LORD your God in vain.

3. Remember to keep holy the LORD's Day.

4. Honor your father and your mother.

5. You shall not kill.

6. You shall not commit adultery.

7. You shall not steal.

8. You shall not bear false witness against your neighbor.

9. You shall not covet your neighbor's wife.

10. You shall not covet your neighbor's goods.

Love and Respect

God gave us the Ten Commandments so we can know how to live a life of love. The first three commandments help us to show love and respect for God. The other seven commandments help us to show love and respect for ourselves and others.

The *Great* Commandment

Once while Jesus was teaching, someone asked him which commandment was the greatest. Jesus replied:

"You shall love the Lord, your God, with all your heart, with all your soul, and with all your mind. This is the greatest and the first commandment. The second is like it: You shall love your neighbor as yourself" (Matthew 22:37–39).

Meet *Annie*

Age: 11

Town: Chicago, Illinois

"Today I was eating lunch with two of my friends at our regular table. As we were talking, I saw the new girl, Caroline, looking for a place to sit. She seemed upset. A lot of the kids in our class have been ignoring her. This morning one of the popular girls made fun of her outfit and everyone laughed. Since Caroline seemed lost, my friends and I decided to invite her to sit at our table. For the first time that day I saw her smile. My friends and I had a great time sharing stories and laughing together with Caroline. I even gave her half of my apple and she gave me one of her cookies. I'm so glad we asked Caroline to sit with us. She is going to be a great friend."

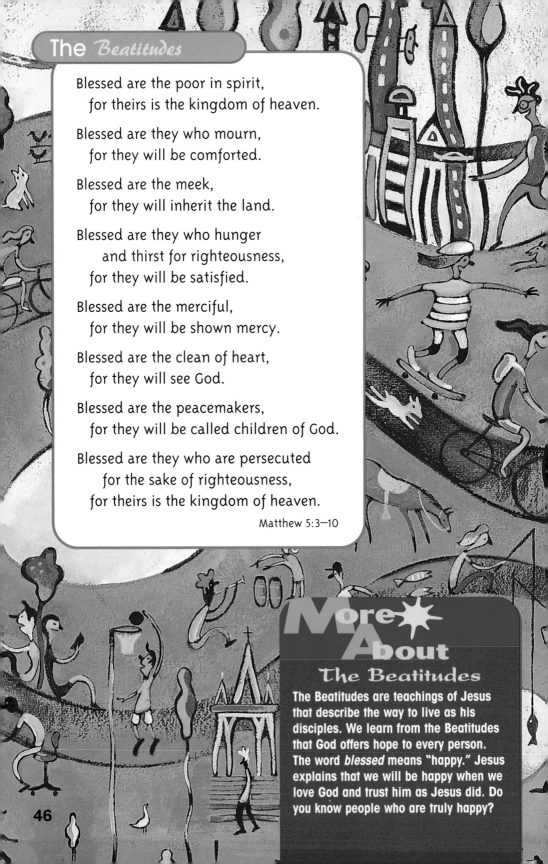

Blessed are the poor in spirit,
for theirs is the kingdom of heaven.

Blessed are they who mourn,
for they will be comforted.

Blessed are the meek,
for they will inherit the land.

Blessed are they who hunger
and thirst for righteousness,
for they will be satisfied.

Blessed are the merciful,
for they will be shown mercy.

Blessed are the clean of heart,
for they will see God.

Blessed are the peacemakers,
for they will be called children of God.

Blessed are they who are persecuted
for the sake of righteousness,
for theirs is the kingdom of heaven.

Matthew 5:3–10

More About
The Beatitudes

The Beatitudes are teachings of Jesus that describe the way to live as his disciples. We learn from the Beatitudes that God offers hope to every person. The word *blessed* means "happy." Jesus explains that we will be happy when we love God and trust him as Jesus did. Do you know people who are truly happy?

The *Works of Mercy*

Spiritual Works of Mercy

Counsel the doubtful.
  (Give advice to those who need it.)

Instruct the ignorant.
  (Share our knowledge with others.)

Admonish sinners.
  (Give correction to those who
  need it.)

Comfort the afflicted.
  (Comfort those who suffer.)

Forgive offenses.
  (Forgive those who hurt us.)

Bear wrongs patiently.
  (Be patient with others.)

Pray for the living and the dead.

Did you Know?

The Works of Mercy are acts of love that help us care for the needs of others. The Corporal Works of Mercy are ways we can take care of the physical and material needs of others. The Spiritual Works of Mercy are ways we can serve the needs of people's hearts, minds, and souls. We give witness to Jesus when we perform the Works of Mercy.

Corporal Works of Mercy

Feed the hungry.

Give drink to the thirsty.

Clothe the naked.

Shelter the homeless.

Visit the sick.

Visit the imprisoned.

Bury the dead.

HOSPITAL TOY DRIVE

The Precepts *of the Church*

1. You shall attend Mass on Sundays and on holy days of obligation and rest from servile labor.

2. You shall confess your sins at least once a year.

3. You shall receive the Sacrament of the Eucharist at least during the Easter season.

4. You shall observe the days of fasting and abstinence established by the Church.

5. You shall help to provide for the needs of the Church.

Why do we need Them?

The pope and bishops have established some laws to help us know and fulfill our responsibilities as members of the Church. These laws are called the *precepts of the Church*. They teach us how we should act as members of the Church. They help the Church to grow together in Christ.

Holy Days of Obligation

Here are the holy days of obligation that the Church in the United States celebrates.

Solemnity of Mary, Mother of God
(January 1)

Ascension
(when celebrated on Thursday during the Easter season)

Assumption of Mary
(August 15)

All Saints' Day
(November 1)

Immaculate Conception
(December 8)

Christmas
(December 25)

Catholic Social Teaching

Catholic social teaching calls us to work for justice and peace as Jesus did. Jesus' life and teaching are the foundation of Catholic social teaching.

Life and Dignity of the Human Person
Human life is sacred because it is a gift from God. Because we are all God's children, we all share the same human dignity—our worth and value. Our dignity comes from being made in the image and likeness of God. This dignity makes us equal.

Call to Family, Community, and Participation
The family is the basic community in society. In the family we grow and learn values. We learn what it means to be part of a group. Families contribute to society in many ways. As Catholics we are involved in our family life and community.

Rights and Responsibilities of the Human Person
Every person has a fundamental God-given right to life: faith and family, work and education, health care and housing. We also have a responsibility to others and to society. We work to make sure the rights of all people are being protected.

Option for the Poor and Vulnerable
As Catholics we have a special obligation to help those who are poor and in need. This includes those who cannot protect themselves because of their age or their health.

Dignity of Work and the Rights of Workers
There is value in all work. Our work is a sign of our participation in God's work of creation. People have the right to decent work, just wages, safe working conditions, and to participate in decisions about their work.

Solidarity of the Human Family
Solidarity is a commitment to unity that binds members of a group together. Each of us is a member of the one human family. The human family includes people of all racial, cultural, and religious backgrounds. As Catholics we all suffer when one part of the human family suffers. When we act to ease the sufferings of others we are in union with them.

Care for God's Creation
God created us to be stewards, or caretakers, of his creation. We must care for and respect the environment. We have to protect it for future generations. When we care for creation, we show respect for God the Creator.

The Rosary

The rosary is a devotional prayer in which we remember events in the lives of Jesus and Mary. To pray a rosary we can use a set of beads arranged in a circle. The rosary beads begin with a cross followed by one large bead and three small ones. The next large bead (just before the medal) begins the first "decade." Each decade consists of one large bead followed by ten smaller beads.

Use the rosary beads to pray the rosary beginning with the Sign of the Cross, reciting the Apostles' Creed, and then praying one Our Father, three Hail Marys, and one Glory to the Father.

To pray each decade, say an Our Father on the large bead and a Hail Mary on each of the ten smaller beads. Close each decade by praying the Glory to the Father. Pray the Hail, Holy Queen as the last prayer of the rosary.

The mysteries of the rosary are special events in the lives of Jesus and Mary. As you pray each decade, think of the appropriate Joyful Mystery, Sorrowful Mystery, Glorious Mystery, or Mystery of Light.

The Five Joyful Mysteries

(by custom prayed on Monday and Saturday)

- The Annunciation
- The Visitation
- The Birth of Jesus
- The Presentation of Jesus in the Temple
- The Finding of Jesus in the Temple

The Five Sorrowful Mysteries

(by custom prayed on Tuesday and Friday)

- The Agony in the Garden
- The Scourging at the Pillar
- The Crowning with Thorns
- The Carrying of the Cross
- The Crucifixion and Death of Jesus

The Five Glorious Mysteries

(by custom prayed on Wednesday and Sunday)

- The Resurrection
- The Ascension
- The Descent of the Holy Spirit upon the Apostles
- The Assumption of Mary into Heaven
- The Coronation of Mary as Queen of Heaven

The Five Mysteries of Light

(by custom prayed on Thursday)

- Jesus' Baptism in the Jordan
- The Miracle at the Wedding at Cana
- Jesus Announces the Kingdom of God
- The Transfiguration
- The Institution of the Eucharist

Stations *of the Cross*

From the earliest days of the Church, Christians remembered Jesus' life and death by visiting and praying at the places in the Holy Land where Jesus lived, suffered, died, and rose from the dead.

As the Church spread to other countries, not everyone could travel to the Holy Land. So local churches began inviting people to "follow in the footsteps of Jesus" without leaving home. "Stations," or places to stop and pray, were made so that stay-at-home pilgrims could "walk the way of the cross" in their own parish churches. We do the same today, especially during Lent.

There are fourteen "stations," or stops. At each one, we pause and think about what is happening at the station.

1. Jesus is condemned to die.
2. Jesus takes up his cross.
3. Jesus falls the first time.
4. Jesus meets his mother.
5. Simon helps Jesus carry his cross.
6. Veronica wipes the face of Jesus.
7. Jesus falls the second time.
8. Jesus meets the women of Jerusalem.
9. Jesus falls the third time.
10. Jesus is stripped of his garments.
11. Jesus is nailed to the cross.
12. Jesus dies on the cross.
13. Jesus is taken down from the cross.
14. Jesus is laid in the tomb.

Some parishes have a 15th station, the Resurrection, that recalls Jesus' victory over death.

Stations of the Cross

At each station, after silent reflection, pray:

**"We adore you, O Christ, and we bless you:
because by your holy cross you have redeemed the world."**

What are They?

The word *novena* comes from a Latin word that means "nine." Novenas are special prayers or prayer services that can occur nine days, nine weeks or any schedule of nine times in a row. After Jesus' Ascension, Mary and the Apostles prayed together for nine days, from the Ascension to Pentecost. Today novenas are made for special intentions and are often followed by Benediction.

First Friday *Devotions*

One day in the year 1675, Saint Margaret Mary Alacoque was praying. As she prayed she believed that Jesus was telling her about a devotion he wanted people to practice. The practice was that anyone who received Holy Communion on the first Friday of the month, nine months in a row, would be granted special grace at the time of his or her death.

Today, the Church remembers this promise in the practice of the nine First Fridays. We observe the First Fridays by receiving Holy Communion at Mass on nine First Fridays in a row and celebrating the Sacrament of Penance within eight days of each First Friday. We practice these devotions in honor of the Sacred Heart of Jesus.

Lectio *divina*

Lectio divina (LEHK-see-oh dee-VEE-nah) is the Latin name for a way of praying that Christians have practiced for many centuries. *Lectio divina*, which means "divine reading," usually involves the following steps:

- **Read** a Scripture passage. As you read, reflect on the parts that stand out to you.

- **Meditate** on the reading. To meditate is to try to understand what God is revealing. Imagine that you are part of the story or scene. Silently talk to God about what you have read.

- **Pray** to God, speaking what is in your heart and listening to God.

- **Contemplate** by choosing a word, phrase, or image, from the Scripture passage, focusing on it with your whole heart and mind, and feeling God's great love.

- **Decide** on a way to respond and act on what you have read.

More About Lectio divina

Read Matthew 5:14, 16 in which Jesus said, "You are the light of the world" (Matthew 5:14). *Meditate* on Jesus' words. *Pray* to God to help you be light for others. *Contemplate.* Think about the people who are light for you. *Decide* on a few ways you will be light for others.

the Liturgical year

Advent Wreath Blessing

ADVENT

Lord God,
let your blessing come upon us
as we light the candles of this wreath.
May the wreath and its light
be a sign of Christ's promise to bring us salvation.
May he come quickly and not delay.
We ask this through Christ our Lord.
Amen.

Advent Prayers for Each Week

Always begin: Jesus, you are the light of the world.

Week 1: Make us thoughtful and generous so that we can be ready to greet you when you come.

Week 2: Help us to prepare the way for you by being kind, forgiving, and fair.

Week 3: Help us to spread your light and joy by giving freely and happily to all we meet.

Week 4: Let the light of your love shine on us so we can see you today in all the helpless children, in all who have no home.

Always end:
Come, Lord Jesus!

More About *Advent*

One of the Catholic customs of preparing for Christmas is the lighting of the Advent wreath. Traditionally, it is an evergreen wreath with four candles—three purple and one pink—representing the four weeks of Advent. There is a blessing of the wreath and special prayers as the candle, or candles, are lighted for each week.

Christmas Tree Blessing

God of all creation,
we praise you for this tree
which brings beauty and
memories and the promise of
   life to our home.

May your blessing be upon all who gather
   around this tree,
all who keep the Christmas festival by its lights.
We wait for the coming of the Christ,
the days of everlasting justice and of peace.
You are our God, living and reigning,
   for ever and ever. Amen.

Come, you nations, and adore the Lord.
Today a great light has come upon the earth.

Prayer to the Holy Family

Jesus,
you made your own family the model
of prayer, of love, and of obedience to
   your Father's will;
by your grace make
[my] family holy
and make it rich
with your gifts. Amen.

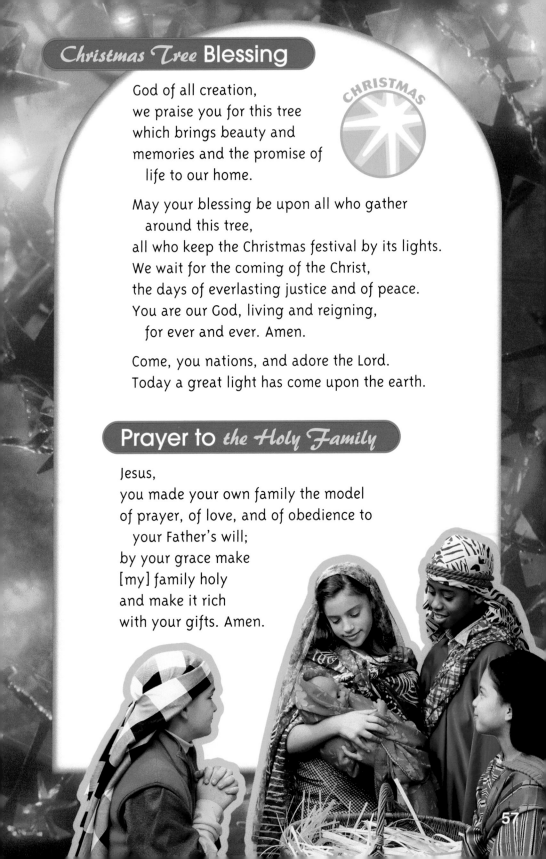

Prayers *for Ordinary Time*

Father of love,
hear our prayers.
Help us to know your will
and to do it with courage and faith.
Amen.

"Make known to me your ways, LORD;
   teach me your paths."

Psalm 25:4

"Every day I will bless you;
   I will praise your name forever."

Psalm 145:2

I didn't Know

Have you ever counted the numbers of days before a holiday or before your birthday? If you ever counted days in this manner, you have given meaning to time itself. By counting time, you have "ordered" it. So too, when the Church observes Ordinary Time, it is "counted time" or "ordered time." Hence the term *ordinary* does not mean average, it means counted.

ORDINARY TIME

Prayers *for Lent*

Merciful God,
you called us forth from the dust of the earth;
you claimed us for Christ in the waters of baptism.
Look upon us as we enter these Forty Days
bearing the mark of ashes,
and bless our journey through the desert of Lent
to the font of rebirth.
May our fasting be hunger for justice;
our alms, a making of peace;
our prayer, the chant of humble and grateful hearts.
All that we do and pray is in the name of Jesus,
for in his cross you proclaim your love
for ever and ever. Amen.

"For I put water in the desert
and rivers in the wasteland
for my chosen people to drink."

Isaiah 43:20

"Yet even now, says the LORD,
return to me with your whole heart."

Joel 2:12

Where do they Come From?

The ashes that Catholics receive on their foreheads on Ash Wednesday come from the palm branches from the previous year's Passion Sunday (Palm Sunday) celebration. The palm branches are burned into ashes. The priest then blesses the ashes by sprinkling holy water over them before making the Sign of the Cross with the ashes on each person's forehead.

TRIDUUM

Prayers *for Holy Thursday*

We should glory in the cross of our Lord
    Jesus Christ,
for he is our salvation, our life, and our
    resurrection;
through him we are saved and made free.

Almighty God,
we receive new life
from the supper your Son gave us
    in this world.
May we find full contentment
in the meal we hope to share
in your eternal kingdom.

We ask this through Christ our Lord.
Amen.

More About Triduum

The Triduum consists of the three days in which the Church celebrates Jesus' death and Resurrection. The Triduum begins on Holy Thursday evening, includes Good Friday, the Easter Vigil and ends on Easter Sunday evening.

Prayers *for Good Friday*

How splendid the cross of Christ!
It brings life, not death;
light, not darkness;
Paradise, not its loss.
It is the wood on which the Lord,
like a great warrior,
was wounded in hands and feet and side,
but healed thereby our wounds.
A tree had destroyed us,
a tree now brought us life.

Lord,
by shedding his blood for us,
your Son, Jesus Christ,
established the paschal mystery.
In your goodness, make us holy
and watch over us always.
We ask this through Christ our Lord.
Amen.

"Jesus knew that his hour had come to pass
from this world to the Father. He loved his
own in the world and he loved them to the
end." (John 13:1)

"Through the cross you brought joy to
the world."

(Good Friday, Veneration of the Cross)

Prayer *for Holy Saturday*

All-powerful and ever-living God,
your only Son went down among the dead
and rose again in glory.
In your goodness raise up your faithful people
buried with him in baptism,
to be one with him
in the eternal life of heaven.

Easter Vigil Proclamation (Exsultet)

Rejoice, heavenly powers! Sing choirs of angels!
Exult, all creation around God's throne!
Jesus Christ, our King, is risen!
Sound the trumpet of salvation!

Rejoice, O earth, in shining splendor,
radiant in the brightness of your King!
Christ has conquered! Glory fills you!
Darkness vanishes for ever!

Rejoice, O Mother Church! Exult in glory!
The risen Savior shines upon you!
Let this place resound with joy,
echoing the mighty song of all God's people!

This is the night when Jesus Christ
broke the chains of death
and rose triumphant from the grave.

(excerpt from Roman Missal)

Prayers *for Easter Sunday*

God our Father, creator of all,
today is the day of Easter joy.
This is the morning on which the Lord appeared to men
who had begun to lose hope
and opened their eyes to what the scriptures foretold:
that first he must die, and then he would rise
and ascend into his Father's glorious presence.

May the risen Lord
breathe on our minds and open our eyes
that we may know him in the breaking of bread,
and follow him in his risen life.

Grant this through Christ our Lord. Amen.

Through the resurrection of his Son
God has granted us healing.
May he fulfill his promises,
and bless you with eternal life.

You have mourned for Christ's sufferings;
now you celebrate the joy of his resurrection.
May you come with joy to the feast which lasts
for ever. Amen.

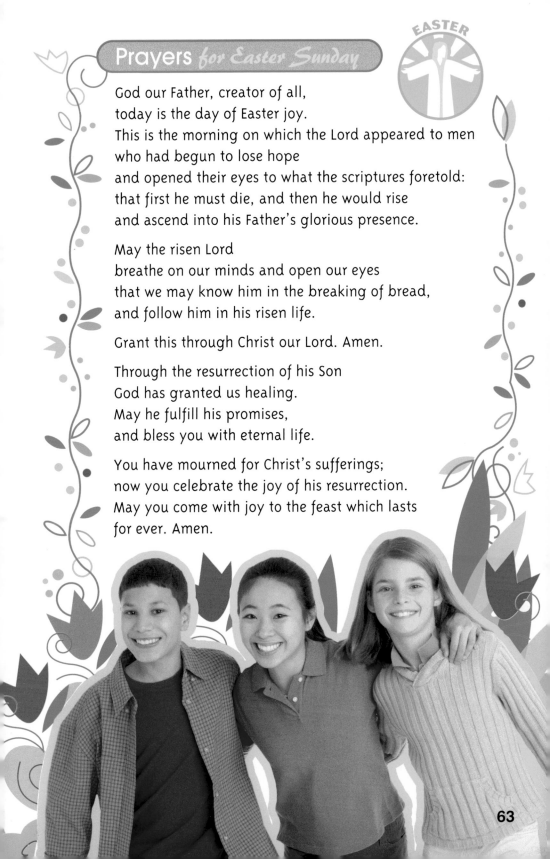

Ascension *Prayer*

Father in heaven,
our minds were prepared for the coming
    of your kingdom
when you took Christ beyond our sight
so that we might seek him in his glory.
May we follow where he has led
and find our hope in his glory,
for he is Lord for ever.
Amen.

Pentecost *Prayer*

God our Father,
you have given us new birth.
Strengthen us with your Holy Spirit
and fill us with your light.
We ask this through our Lord Jesus Christ, your Son.
Amen.